LEAP

Poems By
Jacob Garbarino

Dedicated to:
Every Dreamer Out There

"What's in the way, is the way"

In a life where I am on a constant journey within myself, I've come so far on the feet that I had to learn to use when I came into this world. All the self-doubt that I allowed to crush my spirit when others expressed how much I had to offer; running from the very same passions that placed smiles across my face.

I now understand the journey that must be taken and ready myself for the battles that will present themselves. This is the path that I have chosen for myself, leaving me to do something about the way it ends, my life is about focus and concentrating on what needs to be done to write a story worth telling.

I must become so focused on change and becoming the person that is needed to walk this path. In a life where we've all suffered and doubted our own abilities, I must show myself what surpassing negative thoughts and creating beauty within myself looks like.

Table of Contents

Gilligan

Home is meant for me
Floating in Limbo; Seeking
Purposeful Heathen

Tattered Rose

In the Olive Garden parking lot after giving you the heads up
About the rumor at work that we liked each other
You responded, "But we don't though"
When I admitted fondness and chuckled at your naivete
Your face became a scene of confusion
I was known as the "work flirt"
As everyone else became pigeon-like bystanders perched in
    anticipation
That I would turn beast: rip the ring off your finger, devour
        you to my liking, and pick my teeth clean of you
    Leaving your engagement a scene of mutilated happiness,
    while heathens would graffiti over any sign of love

But only after a couple of weeks, you knew me better than any
    of them did
You knew multiple stories from my teenage years and personal
    insecurities you learned from my poetry
We even had an inside joke that the first thing that always
    came out of my mouth was a lie
And I could tell you had a bad day if you were missing eyelashes
It's something no one else would've noticed, but for me it was
    beauty rendered with pain until they grew back

In the thirty minutes that we were out there the conversation
    transitioned
From figuring out how we could hangout but not give off the
    wrong vibes to more personal stories

You were one of the goofiest girls I had ever met, and we felt
   like best friends
You were the female version of me
Not long into our heart-to-hearts you admitted that you liked
   me too
You being a god-fearing engaged woman, you were in the
   wrong place
And that's when the bombshell dropped
You had veered off from your relationship before and it was
   very traumatic
Even with you learning from your past mistakes you still couldn't
   figure out why you wanted to kiss me
As much as I wanted to, I made us promise that it wouldn't happen
   for the sake of your health
We had to catch ourselves as occasionally we got very close,
   and we goofed off some more
I even sang the few lyrics to "American Honey" that I knew
The night got older and both of us stated that we didn't want to
   leave
You began to hate yourself because the last time this happened
You should have left but you didn't
And you knew your fiancé trusted you but, in that moment, you
   didn't trust yourself
We would spend eight hours in the parking lot that night only
   with the irony of the sunlight being our curfew

The next night we were out there was just like before
That parking lot became a playground where we could be ourselves
Neither one of us judged the other and we really felt like
   kids again

Your smile became monkey bars, a passage to my happiness

I restrained from making flirty passes but there was just one
thing on my mind, and I needed answers

I broke down and laid puddles at my feet as I admitted after
the first night I felt nothing but bliss and I wanted to tell
everyone about you

And how I even took a two-hour road trip with my brother
just to tell him all about you

And I couldn't listen to American Honey without picturing
you in every line

For a girl I've only known for a couple of weeks, this was all
new to me

I felt insane and quite embarrassed for falling for a taken
woman so fast

And I just had to know I wasn't the only one thinking about
the other all day

You knew you should've just lied right there, but we had been so
honest to each other

You said when you got home, I was all you thought about and
you were singing American Honey all day

Together we decided to burn the feelings with ether and watch
the ashes flow away in the wind

And as you began to pull away and the euphoria faded

I was too far gone, my heart clawed desperately for any sign
that you still cared

It searched hysterically under miles of debris from the
heartbreak hoping to even cradle one last breathe that
spelled out "Love" from yours

I began to ignore you and my responses became a dead-end
    road rolled over with fog, I was willing to just stop talking
    to you in that moment
When I finally did speak, I was just as dead as the corpse I felt
    I had been speaking to, trying to conjure conversations to
    reanimate the feelings
I had finally provoked anger onto your cheeks, and madness
    into your eyes
Followed by the glimmering of tears readying themselves to
    base jump down the side of your face
As much as my ego needed to know how you still cared, the
    hurt on your face was something I couldn't bear, so I began
To confide in you
And you wanted to say I was a bad guy
But you forgave me because in the moment of suffering, I
    wasn't myself

The last night was a funeral we both willingly attended
Dressed up in our all-black server clothing, we built a coffin
    and laid everything to rest

I never entertained the idea of closure, but to pour out each
    other's perspectives was relieving
Every exchange in dialogue was a collaboration of lines used to
    write a eulogy we laid to rest in the parking lot
We still had our fun that night but there was no longer a
    feeling of wanting you for myself
We both agreed that some people are only around for
    moments as a lesson from God
And in an act of character development, I ended it early that night

Dear Stranger,

I'm writing this to let you know the things you probably
    already knew

Even on days when you are in your boxers with nothing to do
    at home and you live in the middle of the city

You still have a view of the most breathtaking beach with her
    smile being as white as the sands

Her story is a book worth reading from beginning to end and
    then reading again until every sentence rolls from your tongue

On her best days, she will be home, her heartbeat will
    crescendo the word love until it's all you can hear

While her presence fills the room, and her essence will be as
    sweet as a vanilla candle burning bright

Even in crowded rooms may her eyes be a window to a
    sanctuary, where it's only the two of you

And when she finally descends to end the day, she is a sunset

All those hours spent in the parking lot, I'll admit I was jealous
    of you

I'm prouder of myself for how it all ended

And as I'm writing this, it's been months and ya know, I'm good

Even in those moments, she was never for me

Her lips never formed a smooch that called for mine, or

While her eyes may have thought fondness of me

Her heartbeat in cadence with every syllable in your

name

Atrocity

With every handshake and promise beget deceit. With every labored breath laid trail for a lie. With every sin, flesh casted away from my bones. Souls leap from my eyes, in a moment's notice they slip my grasp. With no water to bath my skin and no belief to bare a bible, drew upon my untimely death. Death begets a new form, falling through circles maneuvering rings as God once did. Reinstalling every ounce of flesh once lost; I only ever fell and I see many familiar faces in my descent. Landing in the cusp of strong winds. Blown about for eons, drifting through a second chance at life. To be met with judgement and left with a perfect punishment. Never had to meet Lucifer or Judas. Never got to meet Lord God, to whom casted me below the Earth. May God send an angel to a heathen, who was never certain of the existence of Christ. Whom had no knowledge of the sacrifice and forgiveness, who carried sin upon his shoulder, barred slave. To break free with will and journey through the darkness, peering into torment and the screams of suffering. To be guided by the spirits of good out of the jaws of evil and up the mountain. To be met with mercy for the evils I've committed on Earth. Angels offering their altitude as I'm pulled to the surface and dropped at the gate.

Dear Island

While I have sailed many of seas
Thrived amongst many beaches of white sands
With the palm trees and strange fruit
No matter how far I travel, there is not a moment I don't think
    about you

I often think about how the heat radiated from you
As I laid amidst you, pondering if I was ready to settle
I think about the delicate flora that formed from your beauty
Where even on an island I've built a city in which only I can
    call home
You leave my heart with knots
Which anchors me disabled, trying to pull these shipwrecked
    thoughts ashore

I pray the seas haven't eroded the love your banks hold for me
I've been stranded for what seems like months
No navigation to track the heartbeat of your core
My only hope is that your shores call out for my presence

Depth

Every time before I go swimming
I dip my toes in the water
To test how frigid the beast will be this time
Then I slowly work myself through the pool-sized slushie up to
    my neck
Before I am comfortable enough to have fun

Maybe I should've tested the waters with you
Before I unknowingly dove into the deepest part of the ocean

And I can't even swim

Hopeless Romantic

Looking for love in a place where demons collide
As we danced, I could see the pain growing in your eyes
I wanted to ask if you were a hopeless romantic too
Looking for love in all the wrong places
Chasing the ones that will never love us back
Searching under every rock, between every couch cushion

Chasing…

But never realizing maybe the person meant for us is behind
And we should stop and allow them to catch up
Hell, maybe I'm not even chasing anymore
Maybe I'm just running

Tragic Harmonies

What would life be like in reverse?
For a man conflicted within himself
It would be his best bet
A life unfulfilled
Resurrected from grief and pain against his wishes
To relive a lifetime of longing, fetal position in the
    overwhelming presence of fear
Palms reaching for hope inside a mouth full of darkness
The consumption of depression slowly unraveling
The descent prior would be an escalade of hope
The sun will open its eyelids
Demons decay into ash
Frowns revert into smiles
To perish peacefully in the being of nirvana
Now we can press play and ask,
"Want to see a tragedy?"

Living Space

On days when your room becomes a mess
When your floor is covered in Lego-shaped insecurities
And every step onto bare carpet is an "I'll deal with it later"
Meanwhile, you stub your toe on your self esteem
With every misstep comes a little pain
And your bed is your safe place

And that hobby that you once loved
That you haven't touched in months is a gravestone
So ashamed of yourself
You fail to even change the withering flowers lying at its feet

The reflection in the mirror is an entity you avoid
The clock is your worst enemy, especially on workdays
The dresser is a reminder of who you must pretend to be
A photo of your dad is a reminder of who you want to be

Your TV is an escape, your phone is life
And the charger is an oxygen tank

The shower becomes a baptism with its arms stretched out
    ready to care for you
You may shower, but that embrace doesn't last longer than
it must because you feel its warmth is undeserved

And the door…
You don't know why, but the door…
The sun, clouds, nature People
Oh, you hate people
All this freedom, all its beauty
You don't have to live in your head with the world to explore
Maybe there is life in everything you've avoided
With the fears that you've failed to embrace
The peace that is offered out here
Maybe when the sunsets and it's time to come home to the mess
You can grab a broom and find somewhere to start

The Curtain

This curtain is not a cape
This is merely my every insecurity on display

Strung up in the middle of a crowd
With a drape expression, not even self-respecting enough to
    not drag myself across the ground

But there's something poetic about being a self-aware curtain
Knowing inside there is a talent being concealed, ready to perform

But why do the curtains fight so hard?

They're just cloth, borderline see through
With that being said, I find it funny how others see the
    performance before we even see it in ourselves

I keep moving forward knowing one day my insecurities will
    be a testimony
Written to inspire others

I just hope I can Julie Andrews this curtain
Into that Doctor Strange cape and become a superhero

With the world as my audience...
Fuck the curtain, I want to be the show

Tailored

"Wow" was the first thing that I thought
When you walked through those old wooden doors
To Marley's run-down thrift shop on the corner of 17th street
Like a skeleton with years of age on its last leg, but standing strong
Its anatomy, quirky yet very popular amongst the locals
You instantly became the heartbeat for the shop
As if you became the source and the wiring became veins
That carried your beauty and fed the bulbs, making the entire
    store brighter

Your eyes and fingers galloped through blades of hangars and
    meadows of clothes
But nothing ever quite resonating with you
But as if I spoke seduction into a draft in the store
You ran up and cradled me in your grasp as I ballet along your
    fingers

Me, a sheet of velvet held up my two scrawny arms
Despite the size, still strong enough to assist carrying the world's
    burden upon your shoulders
Amidst me wilting atop your hands, I can finally admire
    those hazel eyes that are very much complimented by your
    brunette hair
And that beautiful lipstick-stained smile that pours shimmers
    down my figure
You bring me to the dressing room and I seem to be tailored
    just for you

I bring out every curve in your figure and give you shape in a
    puzzled society
Especially the booty!
You said that I capture you in a way no other dress managed to
    do justice for
I even manage to bring out that angelic smile I feel the world
    has been so desperately deprived of

I understand you
So, there we were like Cinderella and her glass slipper Like salt
    and pepper, okay, maybe that one not so much
It's like we went everywhere together
Weddings, birthday parties, and even girls' nights out
All your friends questioning where we managed to find each
    other
We were inseparable, I know all those other clothes that are
stuffed in darkness are jealous right about now
I was even there for your final evaluation for a promotion at
    that job that you never really cared for
But you knew if you could just get the promotion, you could
    finally have all the freedom that you ever needed
Dinner with that sleezball Mr. Johnson was horrific
I could feel him slide his hands up you, as if I wasn't even there
As his hands rose and laid trail for disgust, I could feel the
    eternal tremble of trauma and fear burning on your skin
With my ears lying upon your chest, I could hear your
    heartbeat racing as we both fought to hold back tears
It shattered my spirit to where if I had threads, I'd have fallen
    off your temple at that moment

The ride home was silent, but you could no longer hold back
    the tears
As my silky body became tissue that helped to dry the pain
    falling from your eyes
Every tear was a forever lasting stain upon my conscious
While every fiber in me wondered why you never spoke up
Is it not that easy? Has this sort of thing happened before?
Your past we've never really spoken of

But I knew nothing would ever be the same after Jason came
    back in the picture
I've overheard the stories you told to your girlfriends about
    how he broke you
Jason, blonde comb-over and that attractive stubble placed
    upon such a dreamy face
How could I blame you?
No, matter of fact I do blame you. For your lack of willingness
    to move on to better
You showed me the true colors of our relationship that night
As I ended up a wrinkled mess at the foot of your bed next to
    his clothes that reeked of false promises
"USPA? What is this shit?! This isn't even real Ralph"
His clothes just as fake as his tongue
I can't explain the destruction I felt when I saw how fast you
    did away with me
For a guy you knew only came around for a fix; he left just as
    fast as he came
And there I was drying those very tears, as you asked why you
    couldn't find the perfect guy to understand you

It was only then I came to the realization that
I'm just another article of clothing
Bound to the darkness to be forgotten

Un-Pleasure

Your river dried into a desert
My phallus transformed into a cactus
You whimpered, "it hurts"
Were you referring to the sex or to him?

Body of Water

I tried to hold you like a body of water
As I watched you run down the sides of my hands and through
my fingers
I grabbed a towel and dried you from my palms
You left me with a puddle to try and understand the depths

I whispered my life to a body of water
To only ever see my reflection on its surface

For a while, I couldn't help but to drown in the thoughts of you
But the pain was temporary The waterfalls stopped giving
And my palms no longer searched for you in the rain, only for
something to drink
The oxygen that you carried and convinced me I needed
No more, I find life in every breathe just fine

The First and the Last

The First Kiss
Was a warm blanket
I took a stroll through the Garden of Eden
And tasted every fruit that bloomed from your tongue
I remember our teeth clashing on the battlefield of entrancement
Even how your face conducted ballet through contortion in
    my hands
For a moment I knew Nirvana

The Last Kiss
Was a back road nearing a "Dead End" sign
With vultures circling a corpse straining for its final breath
Even with our bodies pushed against each other
How did we manage to feel so distant?
My love turned cold when I felt glaciers falling from your lips
It was a bitter confirmation

Harness

I left you in the dust
And watched as you blew away in the wind
I wish I could build a windmill
Just to harness you again

Petals

Every poem is a "love me not"
My book is a rose that stands alone
I pluck away

Scars

After four kids I was my mom's first C-Section
I came into this world putting scars on others
Neither would it be my last

After having lesions whipped upon my heart
I pray to be more Band-Aid

Shia LeBeouf

Amongst a crowd of shadows
I've partied with my demons
Enjoying their company; they helped me block out the hurt
I've walked with a battery-operated smile
But have found clarity within my faults
And empathy for those who've casted stones
As we all hurt

A friend asked me, "who makes you want to be a better person?"
I replied, "I make me want to be a better person."
For all I have endured shall not be washed away in vain
Every day is a chance to find happiness
Making every smile and laugh that much more genuine

Nebula

Pinned beneath my
Gravity, comes destruction
Forming new beauty

Mother

I often catch myself thinking about your smile
You'd walk into the door instantly pouring nourishment into us
With a handful of groceries after working two jobs
That smile was all we ever knew
We'd rarely ever see a tear roll off the face of the woman who
    gave us life
When God gave you that smile, he knew it would be the
    perfect gift to your children
Perfectly handcrafted by God himself, I still feel his presence when
I see your cheeks rise and that grin begin to form
You fed us a smile and that's all you ever wanted in return
Being kids we were oblivious to anything that might really be
    going on
Had I known back then, I would've been the most obedient
    child ever
But home was our protector, and it wasn't our job to worry

When I think about that smile
I often think about how you felt after the door to your room closed
What kind of thoughts haunted my guardian when darkness of
    the room fell upon her?
Working twelve hours a day amidst raising five kids
Battling vices while trying to get the finances to keep our trailer
My mother sacrificed everything for her kids
It would be dishonorable to you if I didn't dig within myself and
    shovel out all my talents

And spread them amongst the world just at a chance to give
you the cosmos
Even if you are never honored with an achievement, just know
you don't need a "Greatest Mother of All Time" award
I will do my best to become a trophy and always give you
something to be proud of
I thank you for listening when I learn something worthy of
passing on
But they will never amount to what I've learned from you, every
footstep I take is yours

On my worst days I still can't grasp how you stayed so stoic
You must be the human embodiment of God
Even as a non-believer I still hope there is a final resting place
Because a woman like you deserves nothing less than Heaven

Looking Glass

The mirror can be a confidant
It doesn't have to be the bearer of bad news
It doesn't have to be a pool of disapproval
Where in the ripples, I lose myself
The reflections amongst glass buildings are an apparition I no
    longer avoid
It can be a "fuck you, I'm doing greater today"
Your smile is a relic to be valued
To be laminated in cherishment
The mirror can be a mantra of "I choose me"

In my reflection, I see a sculpted figure
Still buried beneath the burden of stone
I'm still carving out the man I want to be

Atrocity Uprising

To rest upon the mountain and wash hell from my face to ready myself for a journey to become one with the stars. Spirits sing hymns of goodness. The angels give me encouragement as I march for my forgiveness and for the suffering and understanding of my sins. Please pray for me. The serpent moves at night hoping to bring me back to the dwelling of sinners, fighting with angels wielding broken swords. On Earth my mind was a broken sword battered by my faults of free will, it broke in the end times. Through this mountain's peak may I attain forgiveness from the Father, my forehead bathed in penance, to walk each circle reaffirming my spirit and aligning myself with the divine. I journey through the Seven Deadly Sins being freed of sin, participating with my fellow heathens headed on a path with God. I'll bathe away in flames, forgiving myself for everything. For a journey I've made to become a better person and a leader for someone else. Learning that I shouldn't have to suffer for what was the past, as now is where I am present, "oh what an opportunity it is." At the peak is the birthplace of man, cared for by God himself for all these years, waiting for his children. Christ spoke to me in that moment, saying I've veered from the path of good and strayed into wickedness. God allowed me to walk this mountain in the hopes to restore me and give me a chance to reach Heaven.

LEAP

Samurai I

Sheathe a Bloody Sword
Fire Resting Amidst the Lake
Peace Peers Upon Me

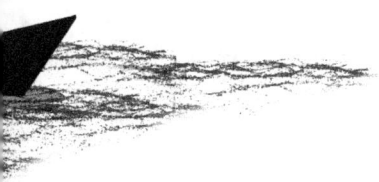

Hi,

My full name is Jacob Wade Garbarino
I was born April 20, 2001
Before you ask, my last name is Italian
I was born biracial and I've been called nigger three times in
    my life
In every scenario my skin was speechless on how to react

I have five siblings: two brothers and three sisters
If my life was a movie
I can comfortably say that love only likes to make cameos in it
Entering right and staying just long enough for me to catch feelings
Before exiting left and talking to the rest of the crew on set

Love tends to leave me being both the scar and the bandage
Applying the same coat of girl that can never love me over the cut
I love a girl that looks like sunset
A girl whose kiss can whisper my lips speechless
Her smile will tell you everything you need to know
And when she tells you the bad that's when you'll know you
    love her

My bookshelf and brain hold an equal amount of valuable
knowledge that we don't use
One day tho
My best friend's contact has an eggplant emoji
I promise it's not weird

I'm allergic to hard work

I often sit down and instantly a sharp pain shoots up my back
followed by me finding the nearest couch to lie in

But I can bench press 135lbs

And I'm willing to debate anyone that a chocolate shake is a
healthy breakfast choice

I dream too big to fit it all in a haiku

So much to try and accomplish, just hoping I can live long
enough to see it all through

Stretching myself thin trying to be everything I've ever
envisioned

My dreams are a beacon of hope that gets me out of bed in the
morning

A lighthouse within the unforgivable waves that gives me
reassurance that I'm doing something right

But somewhere within me I've taken all these dreams and built
a wall

Blocking out my own visions

Not afraid of what I can't do, but the amount of work left to
be done for what I can do

I've come to the realization that I'm all I ever dreamed of being

I just must keep going in order to be the best version that I can
be I hope when I get to where I'm going it's not the end

And that we could lock hands and go on for a little bit longer

I'm still learning to live in the moment

The smiles are always more beautiful that way

The laughter caters happiness to my soul

They say peace is found in the moment

I've often battled with the worth of my presence

I'm stilling learning the value of endearment
I place all my compliments in a jar and try to own them like
    property
Reading them over and over trying to accept what they say
But I can never shake the fact that they still sound like
    questions

I enjoy caramel iced coffee, watching YouTube videos, and
    giving out life advice that I'm still learning to follow myself
I'm a fan of Star Wars, The Walking Dead, and The Boys
Breaking Bad is still the greatest show to hit television
I enjoy music, dancing, and photography
I have a beautiful smile
Even with me being from the South I'm sick of soul food!
In my family I'd probably get crucified for it at the reunion
My honesty about my feelings often feels like a head on
    collision
Hoping I don't say something to soon while hoping she feels
    the way that I do
I'm a ball of self-doubt filled with motivational quotes on every
    reason to keep going
Somedays I feel I don't know what I'm doing
I've been practicing the art of showing up for myself
Which leaves me asking why does everyone come to me?
When they need help or advice
Am I doing something right?

I live my life through writings and "Coming of age" stories
Hoping one day my story will be worth a read
For so long in my adulthood I felt like a child still
I'm finally becoming the man that kid looked up to

My best moments are when I'm at peace
I can't wait to meet my old friend
I hope you get to meet him too
I've come to terms with worst case scenarios
I'm okay with any outcome if I know I gave it my all
I'm still just working, hoping one day I can have that happy
    ending

Father

Rising at 4 o'clock AM
To place the forest atop my scrawny build
Probably 5'4, one hundred and twenty pounds, built like a
  high school cheerleader
I could've stood out there naked and be mistaken for a tree
  branch
Probably just going to bed after hours of playing Call of Duty
But I'll recover some sleep on the way to the hunting spot

When we get to the spot, we use the remaining camo and gear
To turn ourselves into specters that blow fire from their hands
My favorite was duck hunting: fast pace and exciting
Deer and turkey required too much patience for a fourteen-
  year- old like me
Even at that age, the loud noise of gunpowder explosions
  turned a one-sided gunfight
Into a battlefield that frightened me
So you did most of the shooting
Most days we would kill, some days nothing

But thinking back that never mattered to you, did it?
The same safety lectures I had heard a thousand times
The old hunting stories from your youth
Sitting for hours with only birds to sing me to sleep
Critters mounting the body of a napping giant from the forest
  floor

Every dead duck was a smile that stroked happiness into your
    eyes
Every lesson was a piece of you that will forever live on
The woods were a bond only tied through time
I wouldn't be surprised if you took me out there in the off
    seasons just to have those moments

Hair I

Some of my earliest memories were me wanting to grow my
    hair out
My mother was totally against the idea
Cutting it down before I even had the chance to run my ten-
    year- old fingers through the curls
I just wanted to rock an afro pick with the fist
Trying to be on my Roll Bounce shit
What made it worse, she had assigned a barber with zero years
    of barber school experience to grace her youngest child's
    head with clippers
My brother
I vividly remember running away crying every time

Nowadays my hair conducts free fall when it's braided
They acknowledge the growth
They ask to touch it
I say, "we finally made it!"

Milo

My friend's cat Milo is the laziest real estate owner I know
I inspire to be just like him
No money down he has his own castle made of carpet
Lives on every countertop
Eats whenever, sleeps wherever, and has everyone else clean up
    his shit
He doesn't keep his eye on the stock market neither does he lift
    a paw to work
He just purrs when he fiends for attention and gets it
I know felines rub against their environment to claim territory
His head is my palm, caress and claim ownership

Fine Wine

I learned value equals time spent
Love is a currency I hold like pocket change
Jingling in excitement, ready to spare
But I want them to hold me like a chalice
Filled to the rim with the sweetest wine on the market
I'll lie within their fingers and steal the lipstick from their lips
Offering tenderness, I'll listen and spill every ounce of richness
Only if they're willing to pay

Love

I'm not with you because I love you
I genuinely enjoy your presence
You're a taste of sunshine that I pour into my tea
In a life where I've moved so fast
You're a reminder of why I love living in the moment
And a reason for me to smile a bit bigger

Her Lips

Her lips soft spoken
Speaking her heart, puckering
A right of passage

Hair II

To be honest, I probably approached you because of your hair
Blonde, falling down the small of your back like leaves in
    autumn
So transformative
The humidity can cause a blowout resembling a nail-stricken tire
When I go in for a kiss, I run my hands through the silk to
    curl it behind you ears
It falls over my hands like water

This is a "I'll Actually Try to Write a Love Poem" Poem

If I ever actually tried to write a love poem this would be it. Your essence is a spirit that I would happily call a roommate. You're an absurd dose of caffeine that wakes me up in the morning. Even with the blinds closed, you pour just as much sunshine into my day and at night your body makes my bed that much more appealing. When you walk through the door my ears perk up at a whiff of your scent; that aroma that with one hug I'll happily bathe in. Your touch caresses melodic hymns from my skin, as the hair on my arms begin to rise and praise dance in your beauty.

You're a revolver with love loaded into every chamber. With a squeeze of the trigger, I become a victim, spreading my arms embracing every round. Catching every shot with my heart, grasping for my last breath, before hitting the ground, and smiling from the adrenaline rush.

This is the same poem I would have written for the girl of my dreams before I ever met her. Writing poems hoping I could conjure her up from my words, falling asleep thinking about what she might be like, and questioning how many years it might be before I met her. You challenge me as an artist outside of the things I write on paper, because every day is a chance for me to love you in a different way. Your eyes hold parts of my soul that I wouldn't ask to have back and in a crowded room I feel just as close to you. I show gratitude for the things you've sacrificed and feel euphoria from the dreamy looks that you give me. Even from a fantasy in a poem I could never have anticipated the things that I feel when I am with you.

I know one of my biggest flaws is falling too fast, but the truth is I jumped a long time ago. I figured you'd jump too, in hopes that we could come together and cushion the fall. I remember you asking me why you were special and I gave you a long-winded answer, but perhaps my eyes just knew the one when they saw her.

Murals

When you love an artist
You grant them permission to immortalize you
You'll inspire a mural of art forms
For their love for you will never be short of ideas
Your relationship becomes a gallery
The walls will speak forever, even after they've said it all
For others to recognize the beauty

The Voice of An Underachiever

In memory of Cary Allen Chavis

Sophomore year, Speech and Debate
Performing my piece amongst a den of hyenas
Their eyes formed teeth that gnashed judgement
Held up by a calm face, ears perked in longing
As I spoke my voice shivered cold
My mouth sang parables of silence
I had no business being up there
My confidence was low
My voice; not strong enough to carry such a powerful message
But the voice was something that I always admired

Once a fellow debate member prophesized, I'd one day use my
    voice for a purpose
I say "The irony"
You said when I didn't use my vocal chords
It tugged on your heart strings and it felt like we were never
    on the same note
I told you to go
And when I decided to tell you that I love you
It was too late…
It was too late
Too late to say that I wasn't mad
Too late to say, "the fact you feel alone makes it further from
    the truth"

I'm a whisper within the crowd
A channel on mute
My tongue never leaps out of fear that its feet will fail beneath
them

This morning I awoke with a silver tongue
Shaped it into a sword and cut the air with compositions
Giving the village a piece of me they understood
Realizing before my tongue was admiration for the things I
thought were frivolous
No more teeth, their eyes became an abyss in which I poured
myself into
They walk erect equipped with blades themselves

I'm learning that my thoughts are a whetstone
Sharpening in preparation for what I may say next
They say it only takes a little courage to create what you
dream And when you defeat yourself all that is left is peace
I know even in pitch darkness of uncertainty my voice still travels
And with the space in front of the stage, my words can caress
universes
Each letter written on page is a raindrop that forms a river that
may forever nourish

To those that lend an ear
Understand you've done more than listen

Epilogue:

Today I walked into the pet store
I bought a parakeet and carried him out on my finger
Whispered beauty into his ear, "Gilligan"
Raised my hand out in front of me and watched as he flew away

Sunshine Morning

Sunshine greets me at the window
With blankets I cover my head and fall back into my pillow
A robin flaps his wings and sings me a song
Trees curve and tap on the glass until I respond
Squirrels bring me acorns, deer's prance in the yard, not even a
    blade of grass is idle
In a moment's notice, all of nature is awaiting my arrival
I lift the pane and invite them all inside, they back away
Nudging their heads as to say, "today is a beautiful day"

The Page Thinks...

Amongst a crowd of peers
What can I say to be worthy of a second glance?
Profound enough to be remembered

Exhibit

A blank canvas
Paint me with everything you've heard
Project your portrait upon my surface
Tell others your interpretation
Tell me that I'm beautiful
I know who I am

Kain Carter

After his best friend Ike passed away
Eventually the pills stopped numbing the pain
Bottles poured oceans but couldn't wash away the grief
The only thing he was left with was to look internally for what
    could be
With a passion of living life to the fullest
Every night staring into a mirror; searching

Kain told me to never ignore what you feel
But to endure it, you'll need it all if you're going to continue to
    build
There is beauty within all the pain, but you must be willingly
    to do what is necessary to acquire that beauty

I'm a wanderer walking the path that I've chosen for myself
I have a journey and it's my job to make sure the story is told
    the way it should be

88 Keys

The melody is a transit
The chords send vibrations down my spine that opens me up
    like a book
Those fifty-two white keys resembling my thirty-two-tooth smile
All ten of my digits curved, all ready to sing in unison
Still a novice, so I'd prefer we slow dance
Even after hours of choreography, I may still step on your toes
Maybe, I'll close my eyes and see what beauty comes of this

Hip-Hop Saved My Life

With my earbuds corded up, like a 2000s house phone
With my Trayvon Martin hoodie reading "Dreamville"
Cargo shorts with spray paint-stained Air Forces 1s
My hair carefree, just a rebel to the world
"Lupe Fiasco's the Cool" track eight on repeat
Down the school halls I lip synced while my hands ad-libbed
    every lyric
A scholar to every bar as my head nodded as to become one
    with the instrumental
I was a live performance
Orchestrating with all the Cool in the world
I was Hip-Hop

Corpse

I was born to die
Writing is a great form of living
To be a chemist to a body of work
A page that can manifest a portrait
The pen becomes a blood transfusion
I read that the human body carries about 1.5 gallons of blood
They'll measure my work and question how much I've spilled
With slit veins showering the ground beneath me
I'll say, "Everything"
They tell me to stop making everything about myself
But they'll ask to see the scar beneath my bandage
And question the distance that has grown between us
While trying to write a polished book within an unfinished life
Where every title is part of my DNA
Every stanza strands together, tethered to tell a story
Purging my bones of all its flesh
To leave it behind to something that will out stay its welcome
To live on as an embodiment of me
And if Fahrenheit 451 ever becomes real, may it perish a martyr

Few Good Things

You tell me you lack creativity
You blame your procrastination on every possible way you may fail
I tell you "What an imagination you have"
"Only if you focused on the good things"

Photographs

While packing up my home, moving on in life
I came across a photo of my siblings and I at a parade as kids
I swear I could recall this day and how much fun we must've had
We were so young with nothing but innocence in sight
All we had to offer was joy and smiles
Taking that photo, my mother became an artist

I continued to search through the index of memories on file
Placing them up to my ear hoping to hear something
The laughs that were shared, the conversations that were had,
    the food grilling on the pit, or the happy birthday songs
The trips and all the parties
Most of these days I don't recall
Yet I smile knowing those moments they were everything

To My Closest of Friends

To the nights that immortalize smiles into my memory
Until I'm holding a visual album of happiness
Those embarrassing moments caught on video
We'll never allow you to live down
Laughing over the simplest of things
In such simple times we were nobody but ourselves
No curfew on the end of the day
Sleeping on your couch because it's as safe as the bed that I lay in
Who knew a day could go so fast
Without ever wanting it to end

To my closest of friends
The ones I run to on a bad day
The conversations had that no one else would understand
With the family that I chose
Whom I can always be myself around

I hope we never have a final moment together

Lake Charles

Staring at the city from the shore
Where the largest of tsunamis could never wash away
The seashell memories that tinker smiles upon my face
My heart says, "This is home"
My feet say, "This isn't the sand I deserve"

Reality

My presence reflects my past thoughts
Everything in my possession I have justified
Within a valley of chambers that I placed myself beneath
With the head of a concubine who convinced me the vile of
    poisoned I consumed
Were the fruits I should concern myself with
My conscious knows of beauty and gardens where no doubt lies
Where my spirit bleeds infinite through the flesh that it's
    attached to
A pinch of stardust immaculate in any form
And knows the answers to questions with no need
Realizing maybe if I took my own advice, I would love myself
    for it

Samurai II (Ronin)

My mind is a friend
A double-edged sword if not
A weapon to wield

My day consists of
Perfecting my stance, finding
A story to tell

Resting along the
River, striking with passion
Sharpening my blade

Reflections, haikus
Writing poems, In the water
Birds reflect there too

In a constant search
For peace, in this moment is
Where it shall be found

Chapters

March a word like a bayonet
Pierce my flesh, relax my thoughts
While I gnaw on the ideas of a fellow
My fingers grace the spine while my body lies soft

I will begin to idolize descriptions
My mind falling into a world of fiction
Tell me a story that I can hear and that my eyes can envision

My mind will think, "One more chapter before bed"
My lips will whisper a standing ovation

The book will say:
"Do me a favor"
"Read a little to me"

Atrocity Paradise

The trumpets sang harmonies as I walked amongst the cosmic beauty of Heaven. I sat in hopes that everyone can one day experience the divine aura of love that lives here. For a non-believer why have I been granted this chance of seeing what lies afterwards? I sat with the Holy Trinity and was baptized with divine understanding, as I cried a river that bathed the stardust. I was granted life on Earth to take what I had been given and become more than what I was. Just as in Heaven; no past only the moment to be a presence worth a shadow. Every handshake beget love and every breathe that escapes my lungs expels life. I forgive myself for everything that was out of character and for the sins I should have suffered for. Life is only destined to get better if I strive to be more than yesterday.

Orizuzu

As a swan they'll relish in my feathers
As I bathe within their palms
As I flutter a glimpse of story escapes my folds
They'll never understand the folds just as they'll never
    acknowledge the looseleaf story written beforehand
Like the ugly duck of the pond

When I fly away into the trees
My story never papier-mache when I leave
I'll origami this spirit into a boat and sail the rest of the journey

realjacobwade

Apollo Jay